promiscuous winds

promiscuous winds

poems by Noelle Vial

Story Line Press / 1995

Published by Story Line Press, Inc.
Three Oaks Farm
Brownsville, OR 97327

Book design by Chiquita Babb

This publication was made possible thanks in part to the generous
support of the Nicholas Roerich Museum, the Andrew W. Mellon
Foundation, the National Endowment for the Arts, and our individ-
ual contributors.

Library of Congress Cataloging-in-Publication Data

Vial, Noelle, 1959–
    Promiscuous winds : poems / by Noelle Vial.
        p. cm.
    ISBN 1-885266-13-8
    I. Title.
    PS3572.I238P76   1995
    811' .54—dc20   95-36578
                                                        CIP

Acknowledgments

Acknowledgments are made to the editors of the following publications in which some of these poems appeared: New Irish Writing *(The Irish Press);* New Irish Writing *(The Irish Sunday Tribune);* Poetry Page *(The Finn-Valley News); Fishing News; The Irish Skipper; Marine Times; The Works* Anthologies (Wexford); *The Ratpit* Anthologies, edited by John F. Deane, Frank Harvey, Mary O'Donnell; *Full Moon* Anthologies (Killybegs Poetry Publication); *Inward Eye Broadsheet,* edited by Justin McCarthy; *The Humours of Galway,* with an introduction by Richard Tillinghast; *Flaming Arrows* (Sligo V.E.C. publication); *Force 10,* edited by Dermot Healy; *The Salmon; Poetry Ireland Review; Stet* (National Literary Magazine for the Arts); *Cyphers,* guest editor Ciaran O'Driscoll; *The Steeple; Leitir Na mBan* (special issue, International Women's Day); *Women's News; Sense of Place Broadsheet,* published by Poetry Ireland; *Fortnight;* and *Leitir Broadsheet.*

I would like to thank the Donegal County Council for an Individual Writer's Grant; the Irish Arts Council for a Scholarship to attend the National Writers' Workshop in 1983; Co-operation North and The Poets' House for a two-week residency; and the Tyrone Guthrie Centre for a similar two-week residency.

I would also like to thank my editor, Robert McDowell, for his sustained guidance and the Donegal County Arts Officer, Troaloch O'Fionnon, for his encouragement and support.

Finally my thanks go to my family and friends, and to the members of the Killybegs Writers Group.

To my mother

Sunlight stroking the skin and the
promiscuous wind whispering
"Seize the moment. Surrender to the air's
irrefutable embrace. Trust me that today
even seduction leads to love."

Dana Gioia, "Los Angeles After The Rain"
The Gods of Winter

Contents

Part Three: Between the Ice-Cold Sheets

Part Four: Dynamics of a Black Blouse

Part Six: Sea Lust

part one

The Cuckoo Clock House

Tradition

(for Pat Boran)

He holds it up between forefinger and thumb
"I find this slight, an ancient issue . . .
might suit journalism better.

Better stick to higher things,
a good poem
has no opinion on outside matters.

Show, don't tell,
a whisper, not a shout,
an altar, not a soap box."

Talk of beauty is compression.
You introduce the haiku;
microchip poetry
for busy housewives.

The Glass Jar

Put a ring on your finger:
Second last, on your left hand,
And you'll soon see
How liberated you are!

Have a baby:
Stay at home as mother and wife
And you'll soon see
How liberated you are!

Fall into the hands of a doctor:
Bamboozled by medical jargon,
And you'll soon see
How liberated you are!

"Who me? Not me, this is the
    nineties!
Times have changed. We are equal,"
The twenty-year-old Student of Art
    exclaims.
But, foot-fancy free, working on
    "Her Degree"
Deludes the girl from the barefaced
    truth.

For, in the conspiracy,
No woman wants to put another off;
The fact that childbirth

Is like being sawed down the
    middle,
Or women wriggling like worms
In glass jars on top of pine dressers
Where they have stored their
    "Adult"
Because autonomy is a threat!

Who will enable you,
My talented young mother,
To pen your poems,
Or sing your songs,
Or dance the steps
That drum in your head?

Ask the Arts Council
If childcare is a "Legitimate
    expense?"
They'll tell you softly
That: "Up until now,
Our creative women of Ireland
Have waited till their offspring
Came of age, before they resumed
    their art!"

Wombs removed,
Bedrooms emptied,
Husbands gone with younger game,

"Then, my dear, you'll have plenty
      of time to write!"

Do I see bearded poets sacrifice
Their need to breed, their other job,
Their rumbling best-seller?

Now, like a cornered rat,
I stare you in the eye,
Draped in purple robes of privilege
And the ring that we kneel and kiss.

The Ball and Chain Syndrome

Unearthed by accident
From the deep core of the floor:
A huge ball and chain.
As it tore up, link by link,
It became visible, she was a fool.

Not once had she heard it rattle,
Or had she been stone deaf?
Till that fatal day
When she failed, not one,
But every vital function of being a wife.

Grovelling, she relaid the surface,
Buried the rusty chain
And made sure to toe the line,
Because she knew
A silent wife is a good wife.

So, she sucked his cock
And cooked his dinner:
Was content to be peripheral.
Life is simple; he had his job
And she had hers, so he told her,

As she shivered in a submissive state,
Too powerless to find a language
To convey the huge pain
That made childbirth a simple endurance,

And all men's matters more important
Than your own need to have a will.

Of course, we now know
From the wisdom of doctors,
That it's to do with our hormones
And the lack of oxygen in our homes.

Cuckoo Clock House

It looked harmless:
The cuckoo clock house
Designed and built
To live forever.

The floor tiles
In Roman numerals;
A mosaic sundial.

The wife tick-tocked
To the cuckoo clock
As she stood
By the cooker in the kitchen

As the husband free-lanced
Building cuckoo clock houses
For other thriving, striving,
Migrating families to roost.

Time, pounding its seconds,
And cuckooing its hours,
In the name of the *breadwinner*

Valued his time,
His displaced air.
The wife was outwitted
As the day was short
For a woman's agenda.

Dwelling on her sequence,
She took no heed of time;
It was all alarm!
Bedlam broke the delicate
Synchronized cuckoo clock house.

The inventor flew in and out,
Squawking his threatened lament.
The hands of the clock spun crazily,
Waiting for the wife to support
The imposed conditions of time.

Absent Without Leave

At times she was in every room of the house
sometimes she was in all of them at once.
Bits of her sieved in through the walls
melted through partitions.

He said she was never in
envisaged her
out on the town . . .

Her attempts to confirm by diary dates
that she was indeed in the house
did not persuade him of what he felt:
"I could find you nowhere."

The Plan

To add one last, minute detail
The rough plan
Hatches out of the briefcase.

"If this were my house"
The architect humbly offers,
"I would close up the patio door.
A ten-foot sheet of glass is
A luxury you cannot afford,
A terrible waste of valuable space."

They talk in impressive words,
Conceal the extent of the crime,
Drape their big shadows
Over the preliminary sketches.
The change stares me in the face.

On my table glossy brochures
Introduce a slimline door
Like an animal flap.

Block off my spectacular view,
The mountains that keep me sane!

Over my dead body will I be bribed
With solid oak or brass fittings,
A run of units along reclaimed wall,

In cahoots with the architect,
my husband is bricking
me into my kitchen.

The Man of the House

He entered the room
As severely as a whip cracking.
Children and toys scurried into place
A wife jumped to a flustered pace;
Every electric appliance turned itself on:
The man of the house was home.

Cobwebs blew down from secure nooks and crannies;
The doors shook in their frames;
The house inhaled.
The man of the house was home.

The Husband's Blessing

Withholding his blessing,
The husband,
Without moving from his chair,
Blocked the sunlight.

His lips did not move.
The whole room froze.

His hat hung from a nail,
Always wet, or damp,
Or soaked with fresh air.

Yet her face was parched
While her hair longed
To roam wild in the outdoor rain.
Instead, she nuzzled his cap.

He drove her to Mass and Bingo,
Her coat buttoned to the neck,
A spit on her good shoes,
Ample to shake off the dust.

Several breaths of air
were hers for the taking;
Sometimes she dallied to talk to friends,
But always, the engine idled.

She entitled herself to short breaths
Moving ahead with one eye on the clock,
Dreaming of being drenched
By rain, by love, by time.

Creed

Honourable women
Scouring pots
In virginal misconception.

Birthing brown bread
In ovens stoked by love.

Buying frocks
To wear to bingo,
The doctor's and the shops.

Blinkered men,
Withholding the daily bread as ransom,
Inscribed with the blood of their labour,

Opting out behind pints
Television and the newspaper.

Hallowed men!
Tapping us out of the way
With the white stick of the blind.

Who will sort out the marriage—
The socks?
We no longer support the earth God
That keeps us . . . genuflecting.

Bone-Tired Woman

The part of the day that escapes while I
Am thinking, is at its close,
Unaccounted for in the balance of things.

Outward achievements are invisible tasks,
A small bundle of ironing,
Two baskets of wet washing.

The breakfast bar covered in notes towards a poem,
Decaying fruit and unpaid bills;
A tuning out of immediate concerns.

Infinite patience
Clearing space to enable my children to grow,
A safe haven beneath the seaboard

Where loving hands
Squeeze blackheads from angry skin,
Write letters explaining forgotten homework.

All of us under this roof
Immersed in our own activities
Sense a deficit, somewhere in the books—

A feeling of something left undone
Or something yet to happen,
Having nothing to do with time.

A niggling doubt
Undermines a desire to retire,
Count the heads, check the animals,

 Run an eye over the noticeboard
(Pledge to make appointments).
Then I remember
What I've been keeping down—

In the guise of a bone-tired woman
I fall to my knees
Weeping into the last remains of the day.

Annihilate

You asked a hundred things of me at once.
Not allowing me a chance
To hang out my washing
Or sort out a carefully ironed response.

You ranted and raved at who I was
An artless piece of stone;
You chiselled away
Till I lay in a pile of dust
At your feet.

It did not take much of a breeze
To blow me away.

A Chance to Think

Deal with things as they happen,
so the backlog of demands
won't strangle your breath
in the here and now.

Burn your dressing gown,
clothe your body
with a statement—
scream from the colour you wear.

Don't hide behind your hair—
drag it back with a clasp.
Announce who you are,
claim your uniqueness!

Keep a memorandum:
don't block up your channels
with low order concerns.
But most of all—
do not fly through the day
ignoring the traffic lights—
amber is a chance to think . . .

Don't imagine being somewhere else,
a state somehow better.
Gain insight of the world
you have invested in—now.

Empty your mind once a day—
put out the rubbish:
start afresh with a new liner.

Accept everything that comes—
stand bravely before the mirror.

Holy Ground

Nothing haunts in the full brightness;
my thoughts immaculate.
My skin at ease, nourished by love,
flowing like honey through my veins.

The cat slinks past my legs,
a black messenger intrudes.

Focus on the egg-timer,
keep that mind free minute by minute;
nothing can touch me in this state,
no vain imaginings in my dressing gown.
This is the purest hour of my day;
the altar not yet desecrated—
a great ray streams in my window,

The overpowering scent of flowers
settles into my earliest memory—
familiar as the earth,
unbroken as a promise from heaven.

Standard Equipment

I didn't have a multi-chef,
a Kenwood mixer or a percolator.
But I did have a rabbit's cage
nailed to the kitchen wall,
near the back door,
suspended on two brackets.

Pellets of bunny poop
often fell on the floor.

My neighbours and friends
tiptoed past in horror
as they came to talk
about the latest duvet covers
or to ask advice about marriage.

Is it safe to have a rabbit
on the wall in the kitchen like that?
Oh yeah! I assured,
we used six-inch masonry nails!

His Share of Love

The dog crouches,
knowing that the acne outburst on my face
means stress and he might not get fed.
He will not leap around my feet,
frantically demanding his share of love,
like he did as a young pup,
full of yap and mock growls.

His coat is matted;
wads of fur
shag the hind legs
since he stopped his river swims.

He clicks as he rises
out of the walkway of busy people.

His tail trails into the fire and singes.
Reluctantly, he moves.
He blends into the autumn shades
of the unhoovered carpet,
hungry and moulting.

Before the Collapse of Time

By the time you read this
I will have lived
the last hour of a dying dog's life.

It will take exactly an hour
(they told us)
after the lethal injection sears
into the neck of the family pet.

We feel in minutes, seconds;
long delays and empty intervals
clocking up the inbetweenness.

We come down
into the next unsuspecting beat
ticking away,
slower than usual—

We play soothing music,
Pink Floyd's "Wish You Were Here."

An hour is a neat piece of time,
easy to measure, easy to judge,
easy to slip from one life to another.

We know how long it takes;
look over your shoulder
during the rush of love

at the red luminous digits
shifting staidly towards
a narrow neck of time.

The Point of No Return

There is no going back
to my old familiar ways;
no nook or cranny
to hide a slip or faltering step.

No luxurious outbursts
no blaming the stars
no idle thoughts
no passive wandering
no daydreaming
no sleepwalk through the sky.

No change of mind can drag me
dressed up
to a banquet of mutual misery.

No matter how weary the signless road,
the uncertain trail across rough terrain,
clutching straws half the time,
instinctively cautious in a dangerous world.

A relapse, like a breather,
Forty winks on the edge of things,
tides me over into the end of a long day.

Transparent front, like a wispy veil.
You can almost see through me
into the heart of the matter,
succumbing to mythology.

Shells

I do not crochet words
Into patterns
With cold metal hooks.

I am not fragile
Nor does my package say:
"Handle with care."

I am not a delicate flower
Waiting to be plucked
Or swaying with every wind.

At a writers' workshop
I saw women weaving,
Passing the pattern
To and fro: photocopying.
Sexless poems parade safely
Not a smell of a woman
No perfume
No scent to track her down.

What is the point of living
Inside a shell
With your face to the wall?
Botticelli masquerades for all.
Litter the shore of turning tide
With empty shells . . .
Where is the crooked line of truth?

Forecasting in coves
Bearded poets over pints
Baulking at the "Billboard
    Bunnies."

Toe the line
Scissor the design
Elegant themes
Like pots of honey
A vase of wilting flowers
A bunch of still life painters.
The moderator approves:
"These poems could have
Been written by a man."

Poems pondering on mythical
    mysteries
All the witchcraft of our curses
All the secrets of our seducing . . .
Where is the crooked line of truth?

I smell burning . . .
Home-made podium poems
To-burn-in-hell poems
The mentality of a silent wife . . .
Smell these poems . . . perfume
    poems
The scent to track her down.

part two

In Graphic Detail

No Questions

They didn't have a name for it then
When my mother
Crossed the stile into Brady's field
And threw herself down
On the hard rushes to cry
The death out of her system.

The moon lost its significance
Letting the months run into each other
Like an endless road to nowhere

On the way home
She splashed her red hot face
In the almost dried up brook

So when we saw her on the doorstep
Stinging her legs with nettles
We asked no questions.

In Graphic Detail

My mother's first kiss,
was like the slap
of a wet fish across the face.

She told stories
that turned our stomachs,
captured our minds
over mugs of milky coffee.

We imagined vivid scenes:
long-suffering endurances.
The gruesome details
of long labours;
bending the brass bars
of the bedstead.

The pots of boiling water
(for what, we wondered)
the torn sheets—
the sending out for scissors;
screams that shook
the plaster from the ceiling.

Mingy sex lives
were big on the agenda;
the how-to-kindle-
the-dying-flame-back-to-life:
using their hands

in an ancient technique
for arousing the dead.

The secrets, the magic,
the local aphrodisiac:
the placing of leeches
around the sexual organs
to stimulate a sluggish blood flow.

Our eager ears heard it all,
a stolen look
at the Bumper Book of Sex,
long before the first boy
even came within reach—
no wonder we became
nymphomaniacs!

Not a word of revulsion therapy
worked to undo our Lust,
long novenas prayed
for our settled days
kept mammy in the church
for years and years.

Now we are married
bored and faithful,
gathered around our mother,
for more treats:

she tells us
the exact time and place
where she and our father
last made love.

In shocked silence
at the prudes we've become—
she tosses a lidfull
of whiskey into our coffee!

Offer It Up

My mother said, "Offer it up.
Never waste good pain."

"Your body is a temple
Your mind the altar.
Worship no false gods.
Have faith in the constellation,
Your position and purpose is set."

I hesitate no longer
I offer you my one self, my only self.

Stigma

It is embarrassing
to have a "poet" for a mother;
who sits staring out the window
filling the ashtray with butts.

Locks into the study
first thing in the morning;
comes out for cups of tea,
holding the concrete image in her head—

"Can't talk now!"
Her eyes like a zombie;
zooms past the chaos,
holding it and us at arm's length.

It is embarrassing when friends
peer round the door,
see her with one hand on her brow
bent over the old Bishop's desk—
chewing the top of a ball-point pen.

My shirts not ironed,
my bed not made—
dinner cooking by itself in a low oven. . . .

It is embarrasing when teachers ask,
"How's your mother's poetry?"
and everyone in the class looks

at me, as if I was personally
responsible for this affliction!
"I don't know, sir—it's not my scene!"
Shaking off any potential Stigma.

Why can't she be like other mothers?—
I'd never be asked in school,
"How did your mother do at bingo?"
—"She won twenty quid, sir, but she told the old boy
    she only won ten."

Down to Earth

I see you bend over small heads
Tuck blankets around wriggling boys
Lift toys off the floor into a box.

I see you sometime later
Sitting alone at your desk
You open and close a drawer of secrets

I see you consult the stars
Trace their meaning into alpha
Till you meet the old man himself

I see you fall asleep upright
Your neck hung like a crucified christ
Your feet nailed to the legs of the chair.

I see you awake, hung over
The dryness of life on your lips.

Not Seen By the Visible Eye

Her small child knows she is out not in:
A carcass of bones and flesh
Serves up meals and answers requests.

The small child cries for his mother
Pulls at the sleeve of a shell;
He may or may not find a morsel
Of love or a remnant of care

He is a modern day scavenger—
Not fobbed off with an Oscar performance
Or bribed into silence with endless cartoons.

He is watching a vacant stare,
Thinks aliens came one night
And took his real mother away.

He is the barometer for family storms
Wreaking havoc in the front room,
Dismantling the T.V. with a pliers.

Tonight he will use shock treatment—
Jolt mother back into his world!

part three

Between the Ice-Cold Sheets

Policies

So we'll walk the line
Lie under the candlewick
Quilt of many scenes
Hoover up fleas and carpet mites
Hang Mary above the bed
Plant seeds, remove weeds,
Water the flowers, parched
From indecision
Put a log in the grate
Where poverty flamed
Scour away yesterday's stains
Whitewash the walls holding us in.

The Neutral Zone

My bedroom is no shrine
There is no heavy-handed
Flounce of lace,
No silk sheets
Or satin duvets,
No frilly lampshade
Casting scalloped shadows
Around a dim-lit room.

No expensive hum of perfume
Dominating the air
Over mingled scent
To drown the fumes of love
In the last dance of the day.

No subtle art of seduction,
No pose for centrefold
No bedroom policies,
Last in puts out the light.

Towards the Light

After my bath
Your cursory nose in my nape
Attempts to give me love.

I turn frigid
Interpret your move as demand,
Like a flower refusing
To turn towards the light.

I stay closed in the shade
Pretending you are a breeze.

When you settle
My velvet petals unravel,
Moist with dew in a bodiless world;
I spread myself out across the bed.

Sway gently to a different wind
In my own garden of agony.

The Stone Receptacle

Last night your eyes
Did not sweep across my body.

I saw the pupils shrink
The lacklustre of autumn
Stare silently through my nakedness—

Unable to join you at this time
You went ahead anyway
Embracing a statue.

When I awoke
My flesh was grey like mortar.

An Inner Scream of Withered Joy

Once it roamed the earth
Titillating and teasing
Pink with the flush of youth

Pulsating at a sensual touch
Moist, responsive to its quest

Gripping whatever entered
Warming it to eruption
Expelling it when dead

Absorbing the collagen of the beast
Through traumas of birth
It sprang back to serve
Ever efficient in its lifelong job

Battered by life, love and nature
It thins out to fragile
Dried out like a cured fish

In conflict with the mind
It disobeys the scents and signals
It shrivels at the stroke of love

A wreath is hung at the door
No medals for service
No memories for a lost sense.

Between the Ice-Cold Sheets

Tonight you will see your wife
Through somebody else's eyes;
Unmuzzled and hair askew
Leaning forward in her chair
Adding liberal amounts
Of cream to her coffee.

You are given this second sight
A ringside re-animation
Of what you failed to see—

She will feel different, smell new,
Proof of flowers in heaven
As you reach out for her
In your half-awake half-sleep.

She may even cry at your discovery
Between the ice-cold sheets,
Denying herself nothing
In the unfamiliar air you carry home.
Intoxicated with the gift,

You pledge from that moment on
To see what the eye cannot,
To dance instead of walk,
To grasp things midflight.

Tonight you will lie awake, mortified.

Making History

This day has been redeemed
by a final note in your voice,
the sweet song of a sentence
affirming my place in words.

The night wind dies
leaving us huddled in love
rather than necessity.

All night the bed is undisturbed
incubating a whole new slant.

You were freed
to be mentioned in the annals,
while I dispelled the bat
from our room
coaxed him back into the attic.
My name you have just remembered.

The Meal

Slowly prepared from the rawness
Of a brand new morning . . .

I spread a table cloth
Over the burns in the wood
A small, free-range duck cooks in cider,
A bottle of liebfraumilch cools in ice,
The clock ticks louder and louder
Near your arrival, the empty plates starving.

Thoughts run along lines
like, hunger is good sauce.
This will be a feast;
The feast to end all famines.
Our wisdom brings us together
To eat and test our senses.

Grapes wait on a far side-board.
Darkened mountains move closer
Dinner takes an eternity.
A full moon plays havoc
Throwing us off our axis.

The log burns to ash
reluctantly, near midnight.

Soliloquy

The songs on the radio have led me astray.
Cutting the corner straight into midnight
my mind is having a field day, unhaltered.

The old lasso was too slow
the thoughts too fast, too damned wild.
I was standing with my mouth opened

With the trail of people all day.
I was so hot I did not notice the draught
swirling in around my throbbing feet.

A hot whiskey, one sugar and a sprinkle of cloves
had me almost inviting this state of mind.

A half-forgotten song, some ancient hymn
wound its way into the present moment
bombarding my well guarded equilibrium.

It feels like an ailment, perhaps flu
triggered off by the visiting frenzy.

It creeps through my bones
not even a bath stops the onslaught,
the almost burning up of my senses
the walk through a blue flame.

I am the evidence
delivered to death's door.

Metamorphosis

It erupted full of
Red hot venom,
Ready to melt and maim
All in its way;

Temper, heat and force subsided,
You formed your still death
You're not so threatening now
As I sit on you

Warm butt on smooth face,
Moulded to seat recluses,
Employed by desperate souls

Altar to weeping tears,
Surrogate to loved one,
Bodies drape and convulse,
Salt on ancient salt.

Wakes

I am hooked on black glad rags
and the swag tails of inner rooms
where love, the chief mourner
kneeling at our side
remembers moonscent

I mumble forbidden prayers
visit mass rocks
appeal to dark skies
hold sermons, in our name

I cradle a small death
delicately laced
like an unwritten
decade of the rosary

I hear the banshee cry
greet the consolers
with wise words and tea

I light candles
visualize a golden carriage
drawn by six white horses
escorting our grief to heaven
out of our hands . . .

The Relationship

Our minds merged, there is no inbetween
Not since the day the dove came.

Listening below the floorboards
I hear you move into another room
Now I collect my things and join
The never-ending course of miracles.

We have rearranged the furniture
And opened up the house, amazed
At how familiar everyone looks
The resemblance of thought igniting
The light around every unspoken word.

part four

Dynamics of a Black Blouse

Altering Bras

(for Linda)

Waiting for nature
To bestow on us
A pair of boobs
That would fill
Our sister's bra.

Overeager—prayers unanswered,
We become thrifty with needle and thread
Behind the bathroom door;
We measure up our nubile size
And doctor those bras
Down to a flattened "AA."

Parading off to the
Teeny-bopper's disco,
Carefully selected see-through blouse
Won us an award for special effects.

The Dynamics of a Black Blouse

Crêpe de chine,
Black, low neck to the waist,
Barely decent, flat chested vogue.
It says: "Cher, eat your heart out!"
It snubs lover's censuring eye;
It turns its back on the congregation.
Lovingly, it skims the skin.

It jumped off a plastic hanger
Straight into my unsuspecting arms;
Now, it drags me to parties,
Onto stages and the odd funeral.
It doesn't give a damn!
It wears me well in mock courage.

Together, we will thin out and fall asunder,
To lie discarded on the floor;
Threadbare, with a well-spent smile.

To Burn in Hell

The stain of sperm
On a black jersey skirt
The counting of hours until they die
The hasty scrub of carbolic soap
And a glance of budding woman
In a starched nightdress
In a frosted steamed up mirror
Shivering, the words,
"If I should die . . ."
Grasping the silver bracelet
With the special words engraved
"I love you."

The Miracle

Slowly stripped naked
but for the bracelet:
"Be faithful for at least one year."
You unclamped my decorative little handcuff
and now my wrist is cold
in this long winter
of the longest year I have lived.

Its silver beads encase
all my loving
drawn into the soft metal,
for you arranged this scientific miracle.

A Snail in the Garden

Summer sounds waken you
the sound of a chainsaw
already at work.

The sun streams in the window.
Resistance turns you over
to escape back into
the tail end of a dream,
trying to pick up the threads—
familiar enough, because it's an endless dream.

An hour later you wake again
to the smell of coffee.

You look at the sameness of your room
the overpowering wardrobe,
with doors slightly open, introducing
the clothes you might wear today.

Return to the Real World

I carefully choose the wraparound dress
easily discarded after the debut
the high-cut knickers
with the single diamonte diamond.

I shave my legs after their winter growth
feel the gleam of silky skin
excite me towards the sting of seawater
as I wade in for the first time.

For the First Time in Years

My legs dominated the night;
I had cast off the uniform
of denim and Dunne's wool
to wear a dress, disappearing
up inside my jacket
of a different suit.

The dress dragged eyes
away from their pints—
even the drowned fishermen flirted.

At the bar, I disarmed
with my dormant skill
the leech who stuck
as I struggled out of the swamp
with true tales of five kids
and a husband who ate Danish blue cheese.

Berthing beside Fred in his white "Mac"
pretending to be used to such "plagues"
I wanted to tease you
about standing on the backs of frogs . . .
and wringing the necks of frightened chickens;
but I waffled on so egomanically,
never pausing to sip at my drink
or to smoke the fag, unlit in my hand.
So, next time, Fred D'Aguiar, gag me!

I Turn Myself Inside Out

I turn myself inside out
All my seams are showing
The label signifying
The shop where I was bought.

A stranger taps me on the shoulder
"Excuse me, but I think you're wearing
Yourself inside out."

I look in the mirror
Amazed that I have gone
Around like this all day.

Catwalk

swirling
black
taffeta dress
parades
in tiny suede steps

purrs against your haunch
as you pass me to the kettle

a dress rehearsal
for a dinner dance
needs an eye
a glance

to confirm the wife
who wriggles inside
the cold cloth

this outfit
sexy and raunchy
is available to the world

it shall not
hide out in dark wardrobes
suffering
from the stench of mothballs

this lady
intends to walk the ramp

A Catholic Affair

I will wear a denim jacket
over a short floral dress.

The month of August suits me fine.
You will send me a ticket to fly.
I'll get a dispensation from God
to be with you for two whole weeks.

My alibi might even be
a walk in the Holy Land
to raise money for leprosy.

If our spirits join
towards a sanctifying union
instigated by the grace of God,
resulting in a physical communion
(a loop-hole for interlocking flesh)
blessed by all the angels in heaven
for the purpose of extension
in love's pure name, without spilling
a drop of the sacred seed—then that's fine.

Loaded with this unshakeable doctrine
you can see my hands are tied.
So don't be surprised I'm sitting pretty
(practically a virgin in worldly terms)
looking at the flame-encircled hoops
I'd have to jump through for you.

Instead I dream from a distance
What I'll wear.

·

Don't Wear the Black Dress

Don't wear the black dress,
come in sneakers and jeans.
Wear red underwear
under a vest
as inconspicuous as the rest.

Leave your hair down,
let it tumble
round your shoulders.
Don't wear your sister's shoes
they'll cramp your feet,
a size too small.

Wear translucent lipstick,
a smudge of rouge on the cheeks,
but otherwise wear nothing
to hide the face
I wish to recall.

Come last, when people start to leave.
Tell your sister you'll be late.
Bring something
of yours for me to keep.

Don't be too engaging
in case others linger too long.
Stay quiet in a meditative mood,
swig your drink slowly, near the fire.

Let me watch
the flames burn in your eyes.
Let me have memories
of you to own.

Meaningless Wonder

I will wear ancient lace
draped over the bed
in a delicate seduction.

I will collect a flow
of tulip juice in a phial,
dab it behind each ear,
smear it on my wrist.

With breasts exposed, I wade
in a primeval sea
celebrating my flesh;

At first glance
the visible marks
are the tide gone out—
unveiled pattern mars the beauty myth.

I am adrift
with no reference to cling to
except a stellar sky.

I am a raw cut of stone,
taking time to evolve.

I die over and over for love,
sacrificial offering—Lamb of God
go blindly in my white robe,

bindi painted on my brow
praying to Juno for guidance.

Proffer

I turned down his offer
to set me up as his "*one and only*"
never again having to worry
about being myself.

I would hang out in his bailiwick
stand demure at his side
as soft silken words drape
around my half-starved head.

He would bolt the door
to keep me safe.
He would tend me
like an overgrown garden
weed out my unloved, unkempt life.

He would elevate my status
to Ambassador for all women,
have my tattered robes
replaced with Parisian gowns.

I turned down his offer
of never seeing myself again.

The Appraisal

You think afterwards
that I am someone else,

Because I am real
and not so special.
Your hand did not
pass through me.

You believe
my clothes are saying
something in addition
and you blame me
for your thoughts.

Dream by Dream

He wants her mad, not practical
he wants her without a history
he wants her cut out like a paper doll
from the back of a teenage comic
with a week by week selection
of stick-on clothes.

He will build her, dream by dream
till everything's new;
pliable beneath his fingertips.

In Answer to a Request

My guardian angel
allowed me time out
for good behavior
and I promised
to be home for heaven's day,
where she would
show me off to the world
in my best frame of mind.

You are cordially invited.

part five

Nothing Is Undone

Denial

The world you create
in your dungeon
is the world of make believe,
a place where I am banished.
You cast me outside the city gates
and bolt the solid door.

At times from high hills
I see you at your window.
Your dead eyes, half-mad
in the moonlight, your hands
steadying your weakening step.

From here I send the messages
to change your mind,
to undo your decision to die.
For I cannot enter the ark of love alone.

Dark Glasses

Your unnatural response
is to sit closed off in the dark.
In isolation, you seek a truth,
believing it is outside misbehaving.

Your dark glasses conceal
the suffering in your eyes
but the light still shines around you
desperately trying to get in.

Metaphysical Marriage

Your worst fears are shadows on the wall.
Your sickness is a decision to die.
Your loneliness is a refusal to accept
that I am living in your head
a spark of light in the dark abyss.

Eager to start a honeymoon
already consummated,
a trampled manuscript in a moonlit room,
a white page with a spillage of wine,
the evidence of a joining,
the morning-after stain of truth.

The Ego Temple Burns to the Ground

The truth will dawn on you
When you see a picture
Taken when our spirit joined

Hanging on someone's wall
At a time when you ask
For evidence of the experienced Joy.

The words "Faithful" enter the mind
And at last we are talking
Misunderstandings melt away
All imagined hurts perish as
The ego temple burns to the ground.

A Quick Healing Glance

She stood with her arms
in a basin of bubbles

Slowly scooping up a handful of foam
she blew it into the air
talked idly through the chore,
kept side on as he surveyed
her profile with interest.

Told her story in three acts
until outside the script
she turned
pulled up her T-shirt
to reveal the missing detail.

A long serrated scar
wound down her centre body
ripping its way into her navel.

"It's very erotic," he replied
overwhelmed at her offering.

The Revelation

As you loved me
my crooked nose grew straight
my rough flesh became smooth
the void in me was filled
and heaven came within reach.

Eternity is now and forever
snuggled in the crook of your arm
listening to the sea in a shell
out in broad daylight

From behind the shield
of cast-iron promises,
we will leap together
into a world uncovered
protected by a shell of wisdom.

The Act

I would not budge an inch
Towards the offering of eternal love

To shape our future
In each other's best qualities

Till we are two exact halves
Pertaining to one whole

A pair of ornate dogs
To stand guard each side of the mantlepiece

Admired because we match perfectly
In this arrangement called love.

After Love

She is still warm
like a bird found dead on the pavement.

Feather damp
limp beneath his prayer,
his mouth on her mouth
as she slips further away
beyond his reach.

His last breath, an act of faith,
sends life through sinews
unfolds her wings
sets her to rest on the wind.

Another Life

Another life surfaces,
reclaims my absence
with or without my consent,

Forces me this second
to look it in the eye,
confront the matter
in the light of now.

A mirage or memory
full of potholes.
Who knows the power

As belief conjures an image,
breathes life into it,
scares me out of my mind,

Till I am hanging
by a single thread of sanity.
Attempts to guard a loose thought

Hunt it down and bring it back,
expose it to my reason
before it escapes over the wall.

Swinging an Axe

Outside you reduce your stress level
by cutting logs to last a life-time.
A squirrel watches you sweat.
From the corner of your eye you note
that the windows of your house are black.
No wonder the sun can't get in.

Inside the phone rings
and for one moment you
imagine, but then,
changing direction towards a real thought,
you reserve the dream for when you sleep.

Behind the hard news of a paper
you work out fact from fiction
pride yourself on being earthed.

When order is threatened
you swing an axe.

Short Story (After Married Love)

More themselves than they had ever been:
they walked towards a cattle gate;
a small reminder of other lives
lagging along, inquisitive.

The cows stared. Huge accusing eyes—
is this all a fantasy to you?

Children remember everything.
On the way back he ran ahead.
There was no better time.

The Ascension

I have done my fair share
of sending thorns deep
into the heads of loving men.

I have watched the blood trickle
down their faces mingled with tears.

I have mocked their heroic attempts
and burned their poetry,
refused to let them open a door.

Torn the eye from their heads
in moments of human error.

Counted every bone in their bodies,
even the one up their sleeves.

Barricaded my being with an enormous boulder
and ascended beyond their reach.

A Moonless Night

I retreat now
into the silence
of things not yet conceived.

I leave the moan of conception
and the shrill scream of birth
to you, to invent out of imaginings.

A projection larger than life
designed to scare the shit out of me.

You tell me I am young
I swallow hard on innocence
finding my own way home
in the pitch dark, on a moonless night.

Evocations

Read me like a new language
Trace me back to the blueprint:

If I evade you, hold tight
To the arrangements—
The rendezvous, the room.

Hear my advancing step
Feel me under your roof
Remember, it was not
in words we talked but symbols.

Hold me indispensable
Like a vital piece of jigsaw
Eluding your best attempts.

Gather the evidence
The crumbs the birds do not eat
Observe the notches in the tree.

Prise open the window, look out
Now we see the same thing—
Joined by the great interpreter!

I open my eyes, see you standing
There watching me all the time—
That figure looming
Inside footage of dreams.

Blessed Things

Rushing nowhere
You take advantage of the moment
To start a book you bought
Over a year ago, in a second-hand shop.

You can't get into it,
You reread the same paragraph
At least four times.

The real interest in your mind
Demands immediate attention
And for half an hour
You allow yourself to remember

Blessed things.

Nothing Is Undone

In an ancient dream
somewhere near wakening,
turning over for a last glimpse

Straining to recall that place
which I later identify
as the vast nothingness of elsewhere.

Coming into everything
step by accumulating step
that preserve of the dream
the promise of things
"don't leave me with nothing."

Sweet sweet joy
viewing the seamless scenes
for there is nothing else
as continuous as each day

Where we meet on a threshold
the sleep still in our eyes.

part six

Sea Lust

Mentality of a Fish Wife

I have seen too many
Crab-bitten bodies.
I stood watching
Torsos dragged up,
Recognizing them
By Friday night jumpers.

The big buckled belt
On Bert,
The authentic cowboy boots
On Jack,
The mop of red hair
Of the latest apprentice.

Are you wearing something
Tonight, my love,
As I watch you
Head down the pier?

I sigh with relief,
"Your wedding ring
Has our initials."

The Essence of Sea Lust

Goodbye, my love, the time has come
To close the door on the gale-force winds.
By your side, husband,
I who swore I'd never gamble,
Spun the roulette to watch the dice fall,
The colours a whizzing mesh
Of unforgettable blues . . .
In time, you come ashore;
Your webbed feet reformed to tolerate shoes.

Your clogs blue-mouldy at the back door,
Your pining soul whinging
As the scales dry and flake.
The shelf stays empty
While you foster a new armour and equipment
To seek a sector, to surface a dynamic passion,
To fulfil a displaced merman, unskilled.

Receptive to new ideas,
Like a corn waiting to pop,
Days spent collecting data.
In the night, your body threshed and rolled,
Astern! Astern!
You scan *The Skipper* for an open field;
your eye traces the line of a French hull.
Like a stranded whale, I hear your high-pitched call.
What chance have I against the lure of the sea?

Appearances

I have all the time in the world.

That is why I am
sucking up the ocean
with a straw
while you wait to build
our dreamhouse on the ocean floor.

I see you watching
me with rage in your eyes,
you tell me I am not
who I said I was.

The only things that have changed
are your expectations

For was I not sucking up
the ocean with a straw
when you first loved me
with joy.

The Monument

It was carved out
for lovers since time began:
an unmoving black rock
beyond "Trespassers
Will Be Prosecuted" signs.

A virgin's altar
to lay my single offering.
No mixed metaphors
in the cold-blooded act,

Whipped by an Atlantic wind
away from the nuptials
rowed by a congregation
of hungry oyster-catchers.

The sky was not black enough
nor truly hid my nakedness.
The signs we ignored
warned of the changing currents.

I was not ready for the sharp
stab of icy air, undressing
under your watchful eye,
nor heard the cormorant
nose-dive into the stark sea

On a dark night in history,
as the deafening roar of the waves
applauded our every move
till I stilled the night
like a siren seal.

Abides

I did not really have a say
never dreamed I would need
or plan to be so alone.

So when we led up to it,
the concept of choosing
was not visible in my realm.

I waved good-bye so joyously
because I sensed freedom
brings itself in unharnessed,
slips in early in the morning
and watches loved ones sleep.

There is no penalty
for standing silently on the side
as the effects of love
never wear off but fashion us
further to the shape we attain.

For a long time we stand on a bridge
temporarily lost above the flow
we look both ways seeking signs
clinging to a middle rung.

I will wave to you from here
one more time before I release
you by invitation to my farewell.

The Trinket

You did not believe it was yours
Though it had your initials
Clearly engraved on the back.

You picked it up,
looked it over and found it flawed;
handing it back blank-eyed.
Disowning it made you safe.

It still shines here unclaimed,
a lost treasure,
a denied fact,
that I loved you well.

Biographical Details

Noelle Vial was born in Killybegs, County Donegal, Ireland, in 1959, and has lived there all her life. She is currently the creative writing instructor at St. Catherine's Vocational School, Killybegs. Together with her husband Charles, she has been a director of Charles Vial (Fish Merchant) Ltd. since 1983. They have five children.

Noelle Vial began to dedicate herself seriously to her poetry in 1979 and has won many awards over the years. These include the Hennessy Literary Award for Best Poetry by an Emerging Writer (1994), "Emergent Voice," Cuirt Festival of Literature (1994), The William Allingham Award, The Donegal Poet of the Year Award (1990), Joint Second Place in the Gerard Manley Hopkins Award, and the shortlist for the Poetry Ireland "Sense of Place" Award. She also received a scholarship to attend the National Writers' Workshop in 1983.

This is her first collection of poetry to be published.